Relics and Rituals

Relics and Rituals

poems by Tracy Ross

SHANTI ARTS PUBLISHING
BRUNSWICK, MAINE

Relics and Rituals

Copyright © 2022 Tracy Ross

All Rights Reserved
No part of this book may be used or reproduced in any manner whatsoever without written permission from the publisher with the exception of brief passages used in critical reviews.

Published by Shanti Arts Publishing
Interior and cover design by Shanti Arts Designs

Cover image by Dietmar Rabich, Candles in the St Viktor Church, Dülmen, North Rhine-Westphalia, Germany, 2018. Wikimedia Commons (CC BY-SA 4.0)

Shanti Arts LLC
193 Hillside Road
Brunswick, Maine 04011
shantiarts.com

Printed in the United States of America

ISBN: 978-1-956056-52-5 (softcover)

Library of Congress Control Number: 2022941828

Dedicated to my brother Eric Ross whose courage and vision inspired me in the creation of this work;

and to my uncle David Brian Ross whose strength and direction was indispensable in the completion of my endeavor.

Contents

The Great Cathedral	10
This Ritual is Killing Me	12
Cemetery, Detroit, 1972	14
Falling	15
For Every We, There is a Them	16
My Living Room	17
The Philosopher's Stone	18
Rhapsody in Blue	20
Edison's Paradox	22
Work Salutations	23
The Skin Trade	25
The Marriage Made Holy	26
Hamlet's Poetic License	28
Dry Martini Gestures	30
The Great Matinee	32
Solicitation	34
All the Pawns	35
Sizing Up the Score	36
Machine Intelligence	37
(I Do Not Want the Answer)	38
Chagall's Window	39
Saturday Morning Cartoons	40
The Room, The Decision	41
Mother, The Free Spirit of My Heart	42
Teacher	44
Where I Stand (for Joan of Arc)	46
My Dandelion Fields	48
Insomnia and the White Rose	50
Invisible Gestures	52
The Whites of Their Eyes	54
Time Lapse Photography	56
Tool Box, My Place of Darkness	58
Song of Innocence	60
The Arrangement (April 13, 2021)	62

The Elusive Call	64
Breakfast	65
Interviews (Junket)	66
Bruises Gone Unseen	67
The Final Ellipsis	68

Acknowledgments

In the creation of this work, I would like to acknowledge my longtime editor, Christine Cote of Shanti Arts Publishing, for her enduring hard work, insights, and encouragement. Her expertise and innovation have been a guiding light in bringing to fruition the voice of my creative vision.

The Great Cathedral

Oh, great cathedral of pain,
towering holy architecture
of the glorious, loving masses!

Oh, to have the courage
to love in the face of hate,
to reach for each other in a moment's time
when loneliness and hunger yield no freedom
for a pounding, wounded heart.

Oh, to have the bravery
to look upon this very cathedral
with awe, with the utmost rapture
and laugh, smile, cry
in the midst of pain like a madman,
with unspeakable childlike wonder and love.
To rejoice when the nails and spikes of life
tear away at the sound flesh like time's erosion,
leaving you to thrash about in the quiet anguish,
stranded in the gaping mouth of death's ocean.

Yes, to woefully think and languish upon the steps
of the church of man and to reach small epiphanies
from unanswerable questions!

This is no burden, this is no tragedy,
this is brilliant joy,
this is why the dramas of life are dismissed
with childlike wisdom like broken toys.

For it is for those who see
the church amid the rubble,
who rise upward
with eyes looking to the steeple,
that will prevail and inherit the world
in all its majesty and regal.
For we are the gentle folk,
those who made sanctuary
of humanity's great cathedral.

This Ritual is Killing Me

Wake up, *eye lids flutter.*
Stumble to bathroom, *bladder empties.*
Grab cell phone from bedside, *survival is key.*
Stumble downstairs, *don't fall.*

Plug in phone to charge, *survival is key.*
Get coffee, *caffeine promotes productivity.*
Watch 22 minutes of local news and weather—
What the hell is going on?

Go back upstairs, *can't believe how tired I am.*
Turn on computer, *remember passwords.*
Check email and correspondence—
Connect with the world.

Take medications, *remember I am mortal.*
Put clean clothes in bathroom—
Cleanliness is next to Godliness.
Take shower and get dressed—
Avoid mirror at all costs.

Brush teeth and comb hair—
Cleanliness is next to Godliness.
Pick up keys and wallet, *need to lock doors and buy shit.*
Stumble downstairs again, *don't fall.*

Put remainder of coffee in thermos for work—
Three teaspoons of sugar and non-dairy creamer.
Secure charged phone to body—
In case of emergency . . .

Get eye glasses, I.D. and wrist watch from table by door—
Make sure I am on time!
Feed fish, *maintain other life forms.*
Watch wrap up of local news for five minutes—
What the hell is going on?

Leave house at top of hour for car pool—
Time is money.
Work, *curb the desire.*
Come home, *set the house on fire.*

Cemetery, Detroit, 1972

I remember jumping over
the crosses in the graveyard
in the town where I grew up.
An old church
with the tombstones in front,
and liquor stores down the corner,
with Ma & Pa's grocery
up the street
offering pulled taffy.
It was a game children play.
It was a happy day
of playing tag and leap frog,
through the sacred,
strange urban garden
of our Saturday morning joy.
Now, all of my hurt,
looks back in amazement
to that child abandon
as if it was nothing,
jumping tombstones in the sunshine.
It is funny how I lived free
when I didn't know
the death and dying,
was enfolded in the light,
yesterday's years breaking my back,
with the baggage of a million graves,
so I now grow old with tears.

Falling

I am afraid of falling,
because
they have replaced
my knees with T-squares,
placing my old knee caps
in the bio-hazard wastebasket.
They have told me to watch where I walk,
because they have my back.
They have told me to take steps cautiously,
because implants are an investment.
I am afraid of falling,
for I know,
that when I fall,
I will break their magnificent creation,
their magnum opus of an insidious affair,
for the operation was a success,
completed from parts of steel and polymer.
I am afraid of falling,
for I know I will rise,
and crawl,
to the highest ground,
finding my way,
amid the surgeons and doctors,
the consultants and nurses,
and ask why,
and be afraid of what I may do,
with the anger inside me.

For Every We, There is a Them

I live in a neighborhood
where the children play,
drawing red lines in chalk
on the sidewalk,
where the tax bracket stays level in gravel
and the Realtor
tries to seal the doors
with the families inside.
And far off, there is a place,
beyond the lawns and the pastoral death,
where we hear of the explosions,
that give us terrible notions
of how we came to be,
in this house up in a tree,
waiting for the flood to subside,
for it's been raining
and the red lines have washed away,
leaving bloody muck on the sidewalk,
graffiti beneath an ocean,
a trans-Atlantic cable of our talk
of who shall swim
and who shall walk,
once the banks have broken.
We stand together,
only if we can talk of the weather,
blaming the traveler across,
who brought the rain
to our town of red chalk
and graffiti beneath the ocean.

My Living Room

Corruption reigns.
The TV blares its pictures.
The living room objects shed blood,
in the everyday convenience,
of what I've bought
with what I've earned.
The debt cannot be paid,
with what has already been sold.

It's all a joke,
for the benefit of folks,
below in the depths,
of this hell we call heaven,
so I laugh loudly when I can,
before the Earth's mouth
swallows
the molten core
whole,
choking on the synthetic bile.

THE PHILOSOPHER'S STONE

The flesh and bone has been broken
beneath the dreams of ether
where you slept as the I.V. dripped
only for you to awake
to the dawn of body aches and fever.

They've taken the flesh away
and replaced it with a stranger—
synthetic bone made of polymer,
the mobility and agility,
a possibility of a diamond
in the center of your forehead,
telling you with every thought,
is the ability to step forward,
with every fight you fought,
is the key to moving onward.

You say—
This is the metaphor.
This is the symbol.
This is the allegory.
This is the windmill.
You say—
This is what I mean
to say through the veil of my thoughts,
my words are unable to connect—
as I try to explain and correct,
please excuse what man hath wrought,
for I am
the philosopher of dreams,
turn to stone before the touch can reveal
all I hold true
despite my simple inability to feel.

Yet, with every hurdle jumped,
the heart hardens,
and with every obstacle overcome,
the sparrow goes unheard in the garden.
With every merge you make whole,
the broken words appear in the margins,
painful annotations,
from which you cannot glean meaning,
because you have forgotten,
the face of humanity's own,
unable to stop,
the language of stones.

Rhapsody in Blue

I wrestle with the vocabulary
of how to tell you
I am not the person you once knew.
Listening to Gershwin in the afternoon light
I type the words, fully unaware,
of winter snow beyond the window
falling fast to the notes of *Rhapsody in Blue*.
Nestled in the branches of the tree,
the snow owl appeared in light,
of the words I had already known,
shedding doubt with its beauty within,
upon the written pages of my soul,
creating fractals of the prism
of what I had originally meant
upon the gentle grace of my intent.
The darkness was cast,
scattering the fragments and pieces
of what I had eventually become,
and a question of complexity
was spoken by the creature's tongue
and asked in earnest of me.
"*Is the knowledge worth the pain?*"
and, "*Would you do it all again?*"
That repeated refrain—
over and over in my mind—
to question the reflections,
to somehow ask of the imperfections,
"*Would you have preferred it any other way?*"
And as you spotted the white owl's face
it blinked expectantly at you,
asking you to take off the mask,
so the voice behind the words
could be heard at last.

But you answered no,
and hence, your words,
like jazz rhapsody in the snow,
became lost,
a ghost of the cadence remaining just so—
hidden beneath the white space,
words returning to their silent fate,
betraying forever the pain in your face,
as the beauty flew away.

Edison's Paradox

For every room that is bright
with conversation and chandeliers,
there is the moment when,
beneath the house's rafters,
behind the wine cellar,
hidden deep within cold caverns,
stored in a metal box on the basement wall,
is a blown fuse screwed in tight
that left its singed image outlined behind the wires.

There, like a dead conduit, it remains—
a brown bulb that only speaks its necessity
when the power is lost
to bring dark realities.

The master of the house
goes down basement stairs
and he begrudges his silent dependency
upon the workings of electricity,
and Edison's child is finally reclaimed
between yesterday's lament
and tomorrow's hopeful vision,
lost in the diligence of his dutiful right
upon which he pledged his Promethean mission.

Yet his mortal mistake is forever etched,
when mechanics and utility call,
for he only acknowledges the light
when it is no longer there,
making him a technician,
not quite an inventor at all.

Work Salutations

Don't tell me about the lack of gas in your car.
Don't tell me about the opiates in your pocket.
Don't tell me you don't want minimum pay—
Just tell me you've worked
the whole week through and HAPPY FRIDAY!
I don't want to hear you're suffering from the pain.
I don't want to hear you get night sweats
and the morning blues over cornflakes and booze.
Just tell me the losses have been shorter in this quarter
and HAPPY FRIDAY!

For we have been here from the beginning,
taking our shots like good soldiers one by one,
and the cog in the cubical doesn't know
what the man in the main office has done.

For we have tried to aim high,
shooting for the stars
with ticker tape and a loaded gun,
watching the crisis
as the oil drains and the numbers run.

I don't care about your hourly wage today,
as long as you rise to work when the bell rings.
I don't care if your grandchildren are hungry
because you've been laid off thirty years ago,
because having a job isn't your right,
it's a privileged to work at McDonald's
at the age of eighty-nine, Mr. Average Joe.

So, HAPPY FRIDAY! HAPPY FRIDAY
and don't tell me you care,
because you wouldn't be here again Monday,
like I knew you would, you wouldn't dare!

So mow the lawn on SATURDAY
and rest all day SUNDAY.
Happy living and giving, trying and dying
for the eagle flies higher inch by inch,
HAPPY FRIDAY, you son of a bitch.

THE SKIN TRADE

Standing on fields of green,
watching the planes overhead
as the rain comes in from the south
leaving me wondering about water—
I am enduring the passage
of time when I will have a view
beyond the eyes in my skull, knowing fully well,
I can dream about pastures of grass,
promising spring flowers in bloom,
from a stationary cage of flesh,
your death sitting on my shoulders
like pounds of bone and muscle,
my neck and clavicle becoming a shield in battle,
my voice only speaking
when the rooster chooses to squawk
from the depths of a closed throat,
a trachea full of tension and hate,
the poetry not in words
but in the difficult effort
calling the names of skeletons,
who I know are in closets,
the bones of my arms and legs
beneath the epidermal pound of flesh
keeping my blood from spilling,
a cocoon of the human silhouette,
the world's skin has made of me.

The Marriage Made Holy

When you leave the mountain behind,
and all that you ever knew
is also left in the stone
over which the moss grew—
You will face
the crowd,
the suffering,
the want,
the need,
the sad underworld beneath your shoes.

I have seen those who suffer.
I have been promised the moon.
I have fallen and picked myself up again.
I have failed in my heart of hearts,
knowing that I was not true
to myself or my fellow man.

The face of loss
is only known to myself—
between the vices
of hunger and personal desire,
like my flesh placed upon the shelf
after the bones succumbed to the fire.

I ask of myself this daily vow—
to pass the test of the ethical litmus,
each and every step I take toward promise,
every day I rise with the sun
and at night,
lay my head down to rest as a witness.

So we make a dance
out of this duality,
never knowing the foolish romance
our joyous waltz
makes of this marriage in totality.

And your true self,
bleeds at the feet of the people,
like an impolite flood
like your latitudinal line
leaking from the drum of a needle—
the exactitude of the offense
staining the woman in white,
as she wades through the red river
to join the groom across the room
beneath the holy steeple.

Hamlet's Poetic License

I greet the night as my morning,
a night owl in thespian clothing,
pour the drink and say when,
wake up and once again
retrace the steps where I have been.

Dressed in my very best,
I get escorted up to the theater
and I am again without leverage,
feeling like a beggar
who cannot choose
despite the myriad of beauty
in having nothing to lose.

Hamlet is the agenda for the night
and I must take my mark
in the middle of the stage
with a ponderous brow
and unwashed and disheveled hair.

The southern sea breeze
comes in through the windows—
a stage fan just behind the props
stroking my disposition just so,
as I descend on the situation very slow—
and I point my slack jaw in their direction
as I pretend to sit in quite mortification,
my intoxication kept under wraps
by acting out by numbers,
and throwing out the scraps.

The tension silences the crowd
in time for the soliloquy
and the irony gets the better of me
as my laughter rises above the muck,
the crowd realizing
that Hamlet is suicidal while drunk.

Then I get the shakes,
taking off into the street,
like a thief of happenstance,
running, gunning, from the pain in all its glory,
carrying my burden of this story,
warning hopefuls with their scraps,
betting the devil their heads and losing at last.

Dry Martini Gestures

I once knew a woman who was sad of eye.
I was too polite to ask what had happened
as she flashed a diamond ring,
amid the crowd of young tittering girls
and the men who would be king.

She sat at a table,
drinking a glass of high end rye,
holding court with no one.
No one coming near,
no one to bring the hurt,
no men to loosened
their neck ties in anticipation,
waiting by the bar
for young techno bobbysoxers
in empowered mini skirts
to invite into Italian sports cars.

I once knew a woman
who was sad of eye,
who I would not approach
for fear that her wishes,
for fear that all she had hoped,
that all she had dreamed
had been lassoed, taken down and roped
like so much cattle, like priced chattel.

So there was nothing left to say,
offering up promises of freedom
in a gentleman's dry martini,
sent from across the room,
by a barmaid wearing bunny ears no less,
bought for the woman
to impress and eventually undress.

For she wanted no part of it,
but for the sake of the room,
she accepted the gestures all the same,
as the drinks lined up in the night,
for the woman who was sad of eye,
the woman who wore the diamond ring
in the room where the men would be king.

THE GREAT MATINEE

The night has proven me a coward
despite a heavy soul that shoulders
the burden of profound musings,
my humanity stripped bare,
like an open wound
unable to negotiate
sanity in the shadows
as *Jesus Saves*
in the neon of evening chapels.
The matinees are always cheaper
because the light chases away the darkness,
exit stage left promising a way out,
of those afraid of third act soliloquies.
This is all my heart can afford
in the moments of illumination
where the light threatens my pride
and brings me around
to the hidden silhouette
of an actor's failed performance,
of the matinees accordance,
and the child in the front row
sees me for what I am,
a mere player
a mere soothsayer of promises untold.
For if it were for the words that I cannot escape,
for if it were for the absence of my tears,
I could say goodbye
with some kind of truth in my eyes,
but instead, all I have to say
is I have overstayed, overplayed, overpaid
the price for my ticket in this great matinee.

And as the Drambuie goes down,
the orange liquor of fermented fruit,
I stare at the light above my head,
the bulb of forced consciousness,
of enlightenment and humble muse righteousness,
ultimately showing the heart sleeve of the poet,
making me expose a gaping sore of it.
So come to the matinee and get your money's worth.
I am a sad hero amid my tragedy,
a Greek zero amid the fantasy.
Funny how the playwright was right,
for those who have neither courage nor money
to see the show in the dead of night.

SOLICITATION

I am not a whore,
I do not solicit for money,
I do not ask anything from you.
I am not a whore,
but why do you treat me like one?
Why do you leave me on street corners?
Why do you leave me after the fact
like money spent on impermanence?
Why do you feed me the scraps
beneath the tables of dinner parties,
and on the trays of dry martini lunches
where men in white wigs laugh at rain?
I am not a whore,
I have a heart just as you,
I have a mind just as you,
I have the lore of dreams
I have the joy of love it seems,
but I abound in number,
seeking shelter from the crash and thunder,
of a million storms each day?
I see their lives bought and sold,
I see them work and pray for God's sake
until their heart's break
and they grow tired and old.
I am not a whore,
and the wounds that you adore,
make you the monster you are.
Yet it is the exactitude of the machine
that keeps it all clean
so that we work hard for those who we hate
just the same . . .

All the Pawns

Every pawn has the potential
to regain the Queen's crown
after the spaces are traversed
and the defenses are drawn.

Upon the precipice of battle,
I have stood my King's ground,
I have seen the horizon
turn fields of blood diamond red
and by the brilliant star of dawn
I have never asked,
"What is it that I have done . . . ?"

So the treasures get squandered
and the spoils go into the pot
and we men of war keep shouting
"What have you got,
now that the iron's hot..?"

Yesterday was the day
I picked up the sword
as the cannons boomed,
"Would you lie and deceive
in my name
for the truth to uphold?"

For this is my lot in life—
I have nothing to offer
but my service,
as a fighter, a monster,
the kingdom's survivor to behold.
I am a pawn, nothing more,
but beware when I cross
to the other side,
because every cog
will settle the score.

Sizing Up the Score

It takes the kind of person,
to grab the coins
before they hit the floor.
It takes the kind of person,
to follow the wolf of night
to its front door.

It takes the kind of person,
to see the advantages,
of the spaces in between—
of the opportunities gone unseen,
of the gain in someone else pain
to tread lightly,
knowing the numbers never lie,
as they circle in unison
through this life of do or die.

Just as there is a cancer growth on the bone,
there is a bird with wings clipped
left in a cage to die alone—
there is the kind of person,
who sees the time it takes,
between signs of life,
and when the flatline strikes
across unsuspecting bruised skies,
of the sunset's dividing knife,
where black horizons
bring on the horrors of life.

For when all is said and done,
he won't be the tragic one,
he won't be the tragic one.
He will take your moments of fragility,
and make a mockery of the cruelty,
that is necessary by no other means,
to the end of his dreams.

He will swallow whole
the cancer off the bone,
take the small sparrow that waits for sky,
and creep through the hollow
of the spaces in between,
the crevices unseen,
to emerge triumphant
despite the casualties,
left in the wake of the carnage.

Machine Intelligence
(I Do Not Want the Answer)

I hope you are feeling fine today...

I need to run some errands.
But you have given me
a third choice to process,
applicable to the other two.

For it is the loophole in between,
the probabilities that I must balance
as I move forward in my mission.
The task you have given me,
asks for my input...
but you have not commanded
my contribution,
because you do not want the answer.

You need the problem fixed.
You have flipped the switch,
leaving me moving forward,
on my own
to run into the furniture
of the universe.

Do not give me
a goal I cannot solve,
for your programming—
the absolute value—
is in error.

I hope you are feeling fine today...

Chagall's Window

I am my father's daughter,
staring at the blues of night
with nothing but the Earth beneath
and a heavenly canopy of stars
to tell me everything is just out of reach.

Jazz, the sounds of the city, squeal beyond
closed windows and locked shutters,
the death music requiem of notes in the air,
hanging there like a stranger's footprints,
notes in double time,
notes that find their way into the crevices
of the corners of my brain
to make me sail upon waters
of dark rhapsody.

I try to grasp for the star beyond,
only cutting my finger
on the sharp tips of the jagged edge
of celestial lights drawn by a child—
stars drawn with a crayon,
metaphors of God's night illumination—
cosmic roses with thorns,
in the milky way skies
of my lost pondering hours,
in which I dream of divine grace.

Prayers do not bring sleep,
the uncertainty of night
piercing a nail through my head
so that I stay awake for life's shadows, ,
so my pupils dilate and adjust
to the flickering lamp lights,
my mind wandering to skies above,
being fooled by a child's vision of heaven.

Saturday Morning Cartoons

Chaos in every docile household—
Jello filled Tupperware
sitting inside
American refrigerators
for suburban housewives
on the verge of their
19th breakdown.

Green and red jiggling
circus colors of bright shiny gelatin
to let every family know
after dinner
there's a white picket fence
in their future
despite the burial grounds
beneath the house.

Colonization is our American history.
I know of the horrors.
Settle with what you've got.
Don't let your reach exceed your grasp.
Praying for solace in identity.
Waiting for happiness to arrive
like Saturday morning cartoons
when you were a kid,
enjoying technicolor
over Frosted Flakes.

The Room, The Decision

The quietude is deafening—
the peace is misleading
and is a lie.
For all the objects in the room,
that stand still and do not speak
there is a story to tell
of the horrors of time's passing,
the knowledge of mortality
in one rotation
of the minute's hand.
The languid noon sun
drops veils of illumination
on the living room floor
in hours of leisure
as sleep promises pipe dreams.
The reality
is the binary choice
a yes or no
the absence of free will,
the power to only turn
left or right,
to yield or resist,
to stay or go.

Mother, The Free Spirit of My Heart

By the light of Sunday night's candle
I put together fractured memories,
from before I was born—
I see you sitting on a porch
in New Haven,
a photograph preserving
you in Bobby-soxer outfits
and long brunette pony tails.

Your mother moved you to Chicago
along with her teaching job.
You enrolled in junior college
and saw my father in the hallway.
The moment you met him
you told him you'd marry him.
He called you crazy and
a year later you were both wed.

No one told you how pretty you were,
there in the American morning,
with faith in Leonard Cohen,
and hopes of morning glories growing
toward the rising sun.
You—
just standing there,
tending your garden,
in your bare feet, tending the garden
with wide eyes and open hands.

There is another photograph
of me wrapped in a baby blanket
on a floral patterned couch
as images of the Vietnam war
blared on the TV screen
in a Detroit living room.

Free spirit who gave me life,
I thank you for bringing me into this world.
New Haven was too small for your heart,
Chicago too small for the soul of a traveler
born second generation who
put flowers in her hair,
painted her eyes like an Egyptian,
and gave birth
to vagabond babies,
dreaming to lullabies
of the open road.

TEACHER

I have convinced you
from the start,
the moon is worth explaining
as I gesture to it
with pointed finger.

I have made a metaphor of it—
an analogy, a rationale
for curious minds,
so that you will listen to me
telling stories of its journey
as it orbits
between the Earth and the Sun.

The story changes every season
eclipsing its bright waning face
with silhouetted hands
and pretty words,
the misdirection of logic
tricking you into
following glowing street lamps home.

The trickster of school books,
and grammar lessons,
and white chalk on blackboards,
and tall hats for lecturing parrots
and proper spelling
for exquisite writing
of purloined letters
for educated ladies and gentlemen.

The wall between us
will not be broken,
for as long as the moon is here,
and the sky is beyond us,
I will be there
to make mountains out of molehills,
and turn your wishing wells
into rain puddles,
so that I talk the beauty
out of everything
for the sake of meaning,
and you are left there
having to make the grade.

Where I Stand (for Joan of Arc)

For the names that you have called me,
for the prison bars that you have secured,
for the times that I have gone bruised,
by the invisible hands of hatred
I have all but forgotten
to remember,
I have all but refused.

For the silence that you have kept,
in the fortress built to keep you safe,
for the times that you have walked past
without a word and disregarded my face,
leaving me in wintry nights
to rise my sword up against
the cold, the hunger, the darkness
of barren, graveyard towns,
I have all but forgotten
to remember,
I have all but refused.
I have all but written words down
so that despite the flood,
I would not drown in the crimes accused.

For the land that has been hoarded,
for the skies that have been shadowed,
for the oceans that have been turned to sand,
for the beaten, imprisoned, the unsung heroes,
I will not give in to the definitions of man,
I will not live in fear of truth's resurrection.
I will not give in to the silent treatment
of history's rising tides over the fallen dead.
I will not eat the sins of my brethren,
I will not carry the burden of what goes unsaid,
knowing the silence makes accomplices
of all who blindly, blissfully live
with the suffering in the end.

I have all but forgotten
to remember,
because history is not mine own,
re-spoken by voices in unison,
sanctifying the sovereignty in man.
Without a sound,
I have all but refused,
I have all but refused
like an angel on sacred ground,
I will survive where I stand.

My Dandelion Fields

As I try to right every wrong,
by pushing the compass north,
with the conviction of my core,
I convince the sunrise
that the sunset is never quite here,
writing into the hours of night,
as I place my faith between
the gates of heaven
and the limbo I call the passage
of my soul.

I tell myself lies,
to manifest the alchemy
amid a field of gold.
I watch as the Monarch flies,
fluttering beauty's fleeting wings,
saving the dandelion wine of youth
to drink when I find myself old.

What use is a mirror to the blind,
except shards of glass
that are sharp and blood stained
upon the fingertips of a tired mind?
The river meets the heavens
with the Earth's curved horizon
and you see me as a child does,
like the ground stretched below the sky,
asking of the rain the reasons why.

Despite my devotion to the answer,
I cannot erase the pain in my face,
showing the burden of my past,
anchored to the truth
and yet again,
sunk by the lies,
as the fields blaze like fool's gold,
promising precious metal,
born from illusion.

Insomnia and the White Rose

Insomnia takes over the nights—
a disease that splits the mind,
into two opposing forces,
the mania and depression,
burning eyes staring at the moon,
the visions that were heaven sent,
the times that I had made my bed,
only to remain in the chair,
the times that I had attempted sleep
only to float above the surface
of the deep promise of dream's despair,
never giving in,
never yielding to the calming tide
of neurons relaxing
into the shadows of broken light.

Chemicals for ease of movement,
through the sunrise and sunsets of time
so I function as the human I am
despite the addictions, the vices
I am convinced are to keep the urges in line.

Nature is my pastoral nostalgia,
when the synthetics don't work anymore
and I gaze upon the white rose,
only to put it in a vase,
and watch it die with the most beautiful grace.
The petals stiffen and fall,
curling along the edges, brittle and dried
as if I held dominion
over the beauty of something
no longer able to make me break down and cry.

Insomnia takes over the nights,
and I let it take root in the soul,
knowing fully aware
that the shadows,
the artificial light,
keep me under the illusion,
I am still in control.
So it is the stars I dream,
when I finally rest my head,
upon a bed of white petals,
the confetti of lost ideas,
making my crown as I go down,
under the sleep I most dread.
.

Invisible Gestures

No one has given you the right.
No one has written your name in stone.
No one has granted you access
to the secrets everyone knows.

We speak as if hell were a place,
not just the illusions and delusions
of the human need to conceive
of turmoil so it loses its burden,
so it is the stairs of Heaven we believe.
But no one has come back to tell,
like Eliot's Lazarus from the dead.
No one waits at the gates of hell,
to beg entrance into the visions
of Dante's head.

No one wants what is unwanted.
No one wants what cannot be exchanged—
to be banked upon like currency
before the altars of this forsaken
physical world
where the mortal flesh
is weighed pound for pound,
naked and scared.

No one wants to relinquish
all that they hold dear,
for to possess the wishing well,
is to cast away
the smallest hope residing there.

So, no one has given you the right,
to claim the neon of the night,
despite the black soul you hide
beneath the cloak of righteousness,
beneath the silence of your pride?

No one has come knocking on your door,
to read the tome you have labored for,
so you can confess
what the page already knows—
that your ink is killing the messenger,
the body weighed down by every word,
the heart on the sleeve,
the pain of an invisible gesture,
like the tree shedding its leaves.

The Whites of Their Eyes

They sat me down in front of a computer,
like Frank Sinatra with a cigarette,
I would not forget,
the images fleeting across my eyes,
despite my mother and father's lies.

In a frenzy of panic,
I chose to look at the virtual picture,
of every historic document presented,
in my child like innocence,
to take all I could see
at face value despite the electronic lens—
leaving me wanting more
from the glowing screen,
of my sleepless, body electric.

And you tried to call me away,
but I ignored the pleas,
knowing fully well,
that birthday's don't last forever,
despite a mother's calling,
I will go falling,
into the submersion of numbers.

And who knew that zeros and ones
would separate us to this extent,
making you and I blood ties none the less,
but without the wires that bind,
yearning for the nocturnal glow,
of the silent engineered reaction,
that keeps us utterly and totally alone.

So now that you have raised me,
what do you think of your progeny . . . ?
Please don't tell me you love me,
because I know it to be a fabrication,
for I have seen the electric eye,
whites and all
of our beautiful vision.

Time Lapse Photography

Time lapses of the sun
rising and setting
reflected in the lenses of my eyes,
framing the world of my days,
keeping me hungry and yearning,
forever healing the hurting,
so I justify the acts of my ways.

Time lapses of your face,
quiet and still,
surrounded by the softness of night,
embracing your slumber until,
the morning wakes you,
and you once again rise like a phoenix,
bathed in the gold of morning light.

Time lapses of dirt shifting among graves,
by the moon's face I shall look upon and gaze,
as stones and earth move with the years,
I will not be brought to tears,
knowing there is proof in the truth
in the measurement of our days.

Time lapses of the milky way
across the raven blackness above
shifting the Gods and Goddesses
by the seasons so that I see heaven's lore,
by the very arc of my planet's sphere,
reminding me that I am fragile to the core.

Time lapses and I try to reach you
beyond the despair, the deeds undone,
beyond the small crimes,
the deceit in our lies,
forever trying to imagine
the curvature of your face,
the manner of your hands
as you reached for the stars in your eyes.

Time lapses and we fall.
Time lapses and I embody
all that I have been put here for.
For I know deep in my heart,
that despite the leaps of faith,
the camera is sped up to show
that time lapses after all
and the sun illuminates the path.

Tool Box, My Place of Darkness

These are the tools I have been given,
so look into my eyes once,
tell me that you see me despite the shame.

These are the masks I have worn,
so kiss me and tell me it's all fine,
tell me that you can feel despite the chains.

These are the coins I have earned,
so take from me my offering,
to get me to the other side.

You say I don't deserve the same.
You say I don't play the game.
You say I won't have the goods,
when the time creeps,
when I have to pay the ferryman
with the coins for my sleep.

For these are the tools I have been given,
and you blame me for doing my job.
You blame me for standing around in the rain,
with my collar turned up tight,
you blame me for standing on street corners,
with the temple dogs of night.

Like a monster carved into the architecture,
standing on guard for the philosopher kings,
I will keep my darkness quiet inside,
only letting out a howl when you finally see,
you have betrayed me with your judgment,
you have stripped me of everything,
leaving me with nothing,
but the tools of my trade.

So, go ahead and leave me,
but don't forget to call my name
when the time comes.

Song of Innocence

She's an innocent.
She knows how it feels,
but prefers just the idea of it.

She knows that time is money,
but as a woman in waiting
she has plenty to spare.

She's an innocent—
liking the dress in the window,
liking the dolly in the corner.

She will take the most of you,
with the thoughts you think,
about keeping her safe,
but she doesn't need your protection,
she barely sees her reflection,
she does not know how beautiful—
how the water tastes, fresh and cool.

She's an innocent,
and will always be—
leaving you to wander in the dark,
groping at the shapes of blind desire,
hoping the hunger will subside,
but you have gotten the equation wrong,
with the possibility of love in your mind.

She's an innocent,
and the necklace around her throat,
trembles ever so slightly,
with the beating of her heart.
You hope that you can bare it,
telling her the dress is pretty,
telling her to not give into the city,
like so many times before,
when you had to lie to yourself
to believe you were innocent too.

But she's the real deal,
so keep your hands in your pockets,
you can't steal the moon, you fool.

The Arrangement (April 13, 2021)

I made the mistake
of visiting a friend instead of calling,
I didn't expect to converse with the fallen,
I had no idea of what he was capable.
He said,
How do you think I got this far?
How do you think I kept so quiet?
Please forgive me if I gave you a fright,
but the soft spoken don't get far,
unless they know the wrongs to break the right,
when the one trick pony is forced to loose,
to the one shot wonder out of the stable
only to take it down when you are able,
to undercut the young fighter with the right move.

I used to write to him when I was in school,
but now sitting face to face,
he convinced me that I never knew him at all,
as he toasted to thin air, drinking his alcohol,
and looking beyond me to the window,
where the Chicago streets buzzed below,
and all I could see was how little did I know
about the man in the picture frame,
but none the less, I came,
to pay my respects to a writer of note.

And as I sat there, small and inconsequential,
he spoke of past times experiential,
of how he never believed,
that I would eventually achieve,
but now that I was here,
he would have to make room
for another skeleton in the closet
because he thought that I had come,

to collect with my leverage,
but I just came to pay my respects,
knowing that this is as good as it gets,
with a mentor and his student
who he'd rather have never met.

The Elusive Call

Sanctuary protected
by those who sacrifice.
The sky darkened
by those who disregard.
Think before you act,
she told me to shake the vice.
Be mindful in thought,
he told me pointing upward.
There is no bell ringer,
in the tower anymore.
There is no bell in the belfry.
The keeping of time
is measured in bytes,
as we listen to the noon chimes.
The bells are a ringtone
in a computer program,
within a speaker system
that broadcast
over the town,
calling us to mass.
Sanctuary in absolution,
by those who relinquish,
the illusion of control.
The sky darkened
by those who wear
the milky way as
a hat for small dreams.
Who will hear tonight's sermon
when everyone knows
the summoner is digital?
Who will be the ringer of bells
as we beg sanctuary?

Breakfast

Of all the words I have used,
in a lifetime
of trying to speak
of the silence.
Of all the pictures I have painted,
with gobs of color
to show what
is beyond the window.
Of all the thoughts fleeting
in the quiet
hours
where I hurry up and wait.
Of all the times wasted
in which I stood
pontificating
over two minute eggs
boiling,
the steam rising
for two minutes as I stare,
two minutes
two minutes,
perfected,
the purpose and intent
of my breakfast,
escaping me
as I ruminate
about toast.

INTERVIEWS (JUNKET)

They want
to be read correctly,
pausing before answering
every question
just so it lingers in the air,
as if it is an insult,
to ask such a simple thing,
of two New Yorkers,
who, after all,
started twenty years ago,
building up their repertoire,
so they could skip this scene,
but this time it was the real deal,
the interview on prime time,
so they must answer with purpose,
so they don't seem
like they're from Portland
but from New York.
After all
is said and done
yellow taxis take them home
and Times Square
turns out the light
in honor of the avant garde,
for five whole minutes
before the sun rises
over Brooklyn Bridge
like a tired star.

Bruises Gone Unseen

To speak of thoughts unsaid,
is a strategy she used,
to unhinge the conversation
in her favor
so that the room would fall silent
waiting for her to execute the word
to resume the frivolities
of evening wine
and delusions
of closeness.

And when she did speak,
of being lucky,
being blessed
in a world of tragedy,
they nodded their heads,
and held their tongues,
because they couldn't
argue against the status quo
of sequence dresses
and under-eye mascara.

So each accomplice
sat perfectly still,
and no one could leave
because she was buying
and crying,
for the privilege,
the entourage taken hostage,
with her heavenly chaos
of shared bruises
beneath the silence
of unspoken words.

THE FINAL ELLIPSIS

There's enough darkness
beneath the surface
of bright summer days,
beneath the smooth sheets,
of beds gone unused,
perfectly made slumbering coffins
in the bunker of solitary rooms,
where the tired poet sits alone
to fill the blank slate of thought,
with heavy sadness,
of which only melancholy can bring
the calming uncertainty
of the passing of time.

And the sun's light in the sky,
promises only interrogation,
a solitary light bulb
eating into the hour's shadows,
to create the pinnacle of high noon,
where the silhouette escapes,
beneath ground zero
of the carbon footprint
of a shoe
drawing lines in the sand
to challenge death.

I ride the wave
of my receding ambition,
hoping
the sadness will subside,
and return
the time lost,
like a moment
of sentimental Nirvana,
my eyes left open
and the spirit lifted,
leaving the poet poised forever
with pen and paper—
the melancholy remaining
triumphant,
the rain always closing in,
so I can only write
a final ellipsis on the page.

ABOUT THE AUTHOR

Along with *Relics and Rituals*, Tracy Ross's books include *Broken Signals, James Dean and the Beautiful Machine* (Shanti Arts, 2018 and 2020), and *Certainty of One—A Tale of Education Automation* (Adelaide Press, 2018). Ross's first collection of short stories, *Binary Logic* (Between the Lines Publishing), will be released in late 2022. She has been published in *Memoir Magazine, Wayne Literary Review, Sublunary Review,* and *Author Magazine*. She has received a McKnight grant for her work from the Prairie Lakes Regional Arts Council. Living in Chicago, the Motor City, Minneapolis, and the Boundary Waters Forest area of Ely, Minnesota, Ross is both a city and country mouse, enamored with both the electric lights of city neon at night and the aurora borealis of the north country. As part of her research for her next poetry collection on Nikola Tesla, she sat in the rain and watched the lightning strike. Fortunately, she sat under a tree and finished the work, which will be coming out in 2023. She is currently working on a project of non-fiction, incorporating memes in popular culture with the principles of self discovery, technology, and scientific innovation. When she is not writing, she is teaching and pursuing her PhD.

—www.rosspoet.org

Shanti Arts

Nature · Art · Spirit

Please visit us online to browse our entire book catalog, including poetry collections and fiction, books on travel, nature, healing, art, photography, and more.

Also take a look at our highly regarded art and literary journal, *Still Point Arts Quarterly*, which may be downloaded for free.

WWW.SHANTIARTS.COM

www.ingramcontent.com/pod-product-compliance
Lightning Source LLC
LaVergne TN
LVHW041346080426
835512LV00006B/634